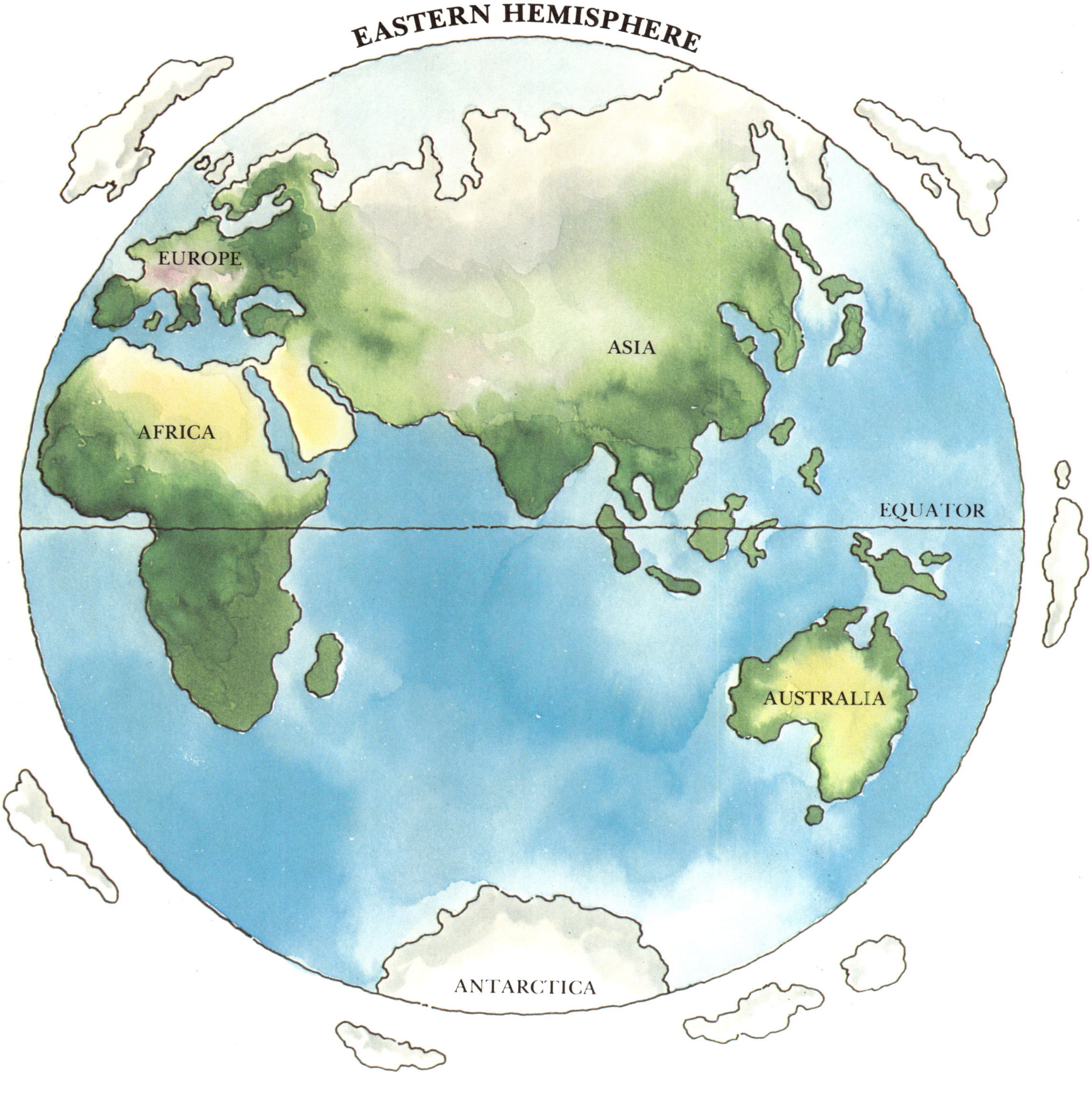

EASTERN HEMISPHERE

EUROPE

ASIA

AFRICA

EQUATOR

AUSTRALIA

ANTARCTICA

Printed in the United States of America.
Library of Congress Card Catalog No.: 75-39569
ISBN. No.: 0-8228-7105-X

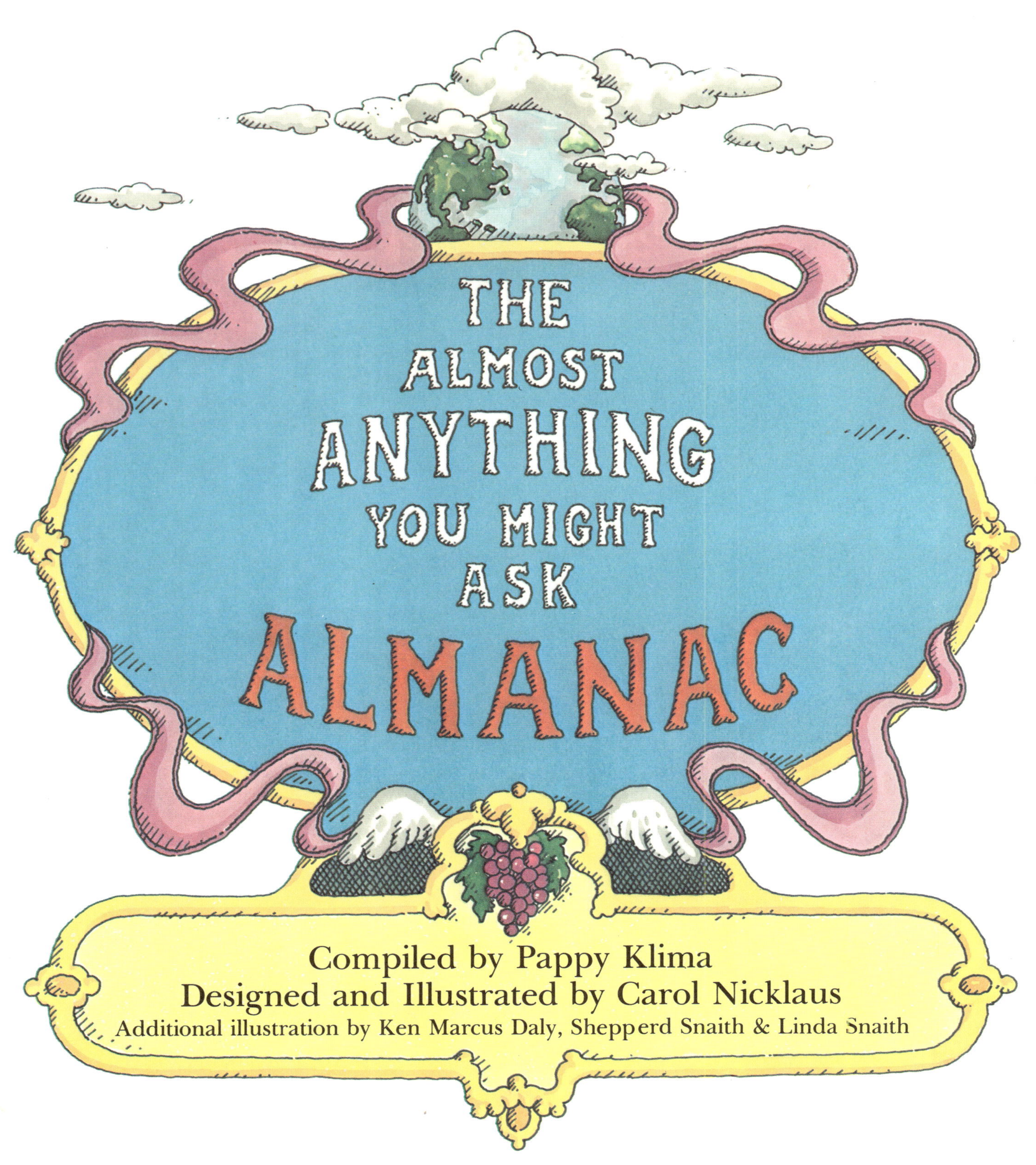

Compiled by Pappy Klima
Designed and Illustrated by Carol Nicklaus
Additional illustration by Ken Marcus Daly, Shepperd Snaith & Linda Snaith

Platt & Munk, Publishers/New York

THE ALMOST ANYTHING YOU MIGHT ASK ALMANAC

Winter **January** • Snow facts & fun • Aquarius • New Year's • The Gold Rush • Emancipation Proclamation • Oil! • Are you cold? • **February** • Tips for the Human Hibernator • Odd Animal Facts • Pisces • Groundhog Day • Leap Year • Boy Scouts • St. Valentine's • **March** • First Signs of Spring • Earthquakes • Aries • Girl Scouts • St. Patrick's • Peculiar Laws • The Zodiac

Spring **April** • Sprouting • Taurus Arbor Day • Pony Express • April Fool • **May** • Worms • Gemini • Memorial Day • Mother's Day • About the Lusitania & Other Disasters • Lindbergh flies • Wildflowers • **June** • Wedding lore • Cancer • Napoleon • Go Fly a Kite • Weather Signs • Heavy Weather & Self Defense •

Summer **July** • Thunder & Lightning • Leo • First Moon Landing • Old Fashioned Fourth • **August** • Garlic Saves • Virgo • Women Vote • Columbus Sails • Friendship Day • At the Seashore • **September** • Why School? • Labor Day • Great Fire of London • Star Spangled Banner • The Foot • Apples • Superstitions •

Fall **October** • Jack-o-Lanterns • Scorpio • Columbus Lands • Stock Market Crashes • Halloween • Witches • **November** • Elections • Sagitarrius • Gettysburg Address • Stanley Finds Livingstone • First Thanksgiving • **December** • Season's Greetings • Capricorn • Boston Teaparty • Washington Crosses Delaware •

Winter

When the sun strikes the earth 23½ degrees south of the equator, it is winter here in the northern half of the world, while it is summer in the southern half. Winter comes from a word that means, "to make wet." Winter is the wettest of all seasons. When the temperature drops below freezing, the wetness turns to frost and snow. If the calendar didn't tell you so on December 22, you would still know that it is winter. The morning dew has turned to frost. The trees are bare. The grass is dry. You know it is winter because dogs' and cats' coats have grown shaggy, squirrels' tails bushy, ant hills high. For many people and many animals, winter is a time to take shelter, to rest or to hibernate. But for some people and some animals, winter is a time to be out in the snow. In addition to the tracks of skis, snowshoes, boots, galoshes, snowmobiles, sleighs, and skates, the tracks of animals in the snow are a sure sign that not everybody sleeps the winter away. Let's make tracks now into the months of winter, starting with January.

Rabbit
Bird
Opossum
Bear
Raccoon
Squirrel

January has 31 days

January is the month when winter is still fresh and new and interesting. January brings all kinds of snow, from snow that melts as soon as it touches the ground (disappointing snow), to snow that falls in high winds called blizzards (no school snow). For more about snow, read below.

SNOW

When it is cool and overcast and the air is dry, the snow is powdery and makes for poor packing. When the sun shines and the air is moist, it is good packing. Flurries, blizzards, powder, drifts, good packing, poor packing—these are some of the words we use to describe snow. Where it snows almost all the time, the Eskimoes have over 100 words to describe snow. We don't have nearly as many words to describe snow, but we do have ever so many good things to do with it.

What you do with snow has a lot to do with whether it is good packing or poor packing. When it is good packing, you can do almost anything. Almost anything that you do with modeling clay, you can do with good-packing snow. You can mold it into snow people, snow forts, snow castles, snow statues. You can roll it into giant balls and shovel it into mountains. All it takes is a pair of waterproof mittens and some imagination. When the snow is poor packing, you can make snow angels, pour syrup into a clean patch and make ice pops. You can catch snowflakes on black paper and examine the flakes. Each flake is a perfect six-sided figure, yet each is different from the others.

And of course, you can always make snowballs. Instead of throwing them, why not store one or two in the freezer for some hot summer's day—a souvenir of the wintertime.

Symbols

January's flower is the **carnation,** a spice-scented flower that grows in white and shades of red. The birthstone for January is the **garnet,** a red stone representing fidelity.

Aquarius

the water carrier
Jan. 20 - Feb. 19

People born under the sign of Aquarius are energetic and emotional. More famous people were born under this sign than under any other. Aquarians are known to dress in a peculiar fashion. They are restless, curious, pleasing and a lot of fun to be with.*

Famous people born in Aquarius:
Wolfgang Mozart, composer, born 1756.
Franklin Roosevelt, President, born 1882.
George "Babe" Ruth, baseball player, born 1895.

Friends' birthdays:

*Remember to swallow with grain of salt, when necessary.

Ken Marcus Daly

January Past

Gold Fever

James Marshall discovered gold at Sutter's Mill, California. By January 1849, thousands of prospectors had rushed West to hunt, pan, pick and dig for gold.

Black Gold

Drillers hit the first oil deposit ever found in Texas, causing a "gusher" two stories high to leap into the sky.

People Freed

Over three million people were freed when President Lincoln issued the Emancipation Proclamation on January 1, 1863. It set free all slaves in the rebellious southern states of America.

Holidays

New Year's Day—January 1
Battle of New Orleans Day (in Louisiana)—January 8
Inauguration Day—January 20, every four years as a president comes into office.
Three Kings' Day (in Puerto Rico)—January 6
Martin Luther King's Birthday—January 15

And

USE THIS SPACE TO WRITE IN YOUR FAVORITE JANUARY DAYS.

When the frost is on the pumpkin and the first skim ice forms at the edges of ponds, it is time to hibernate. Frogs bury themselves in the leaves at the bottoms of ponds. Snakes crawl into caves. Butterflies head for hollow logs. Bears retire to their dens. Some squirrels build themselves nests with double-wall insulation.

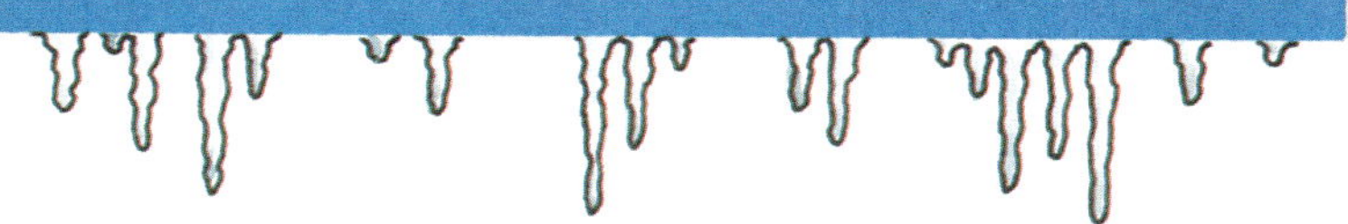

Those creatures who don't hibernate—like dogs and cats and other squirrels—grow long, shaggy coats. Many birds simply fly south where it is summer.

For those of us who can't hibernate, grow fur, or fly south, winter is the time to keep out the cold.

People have been struggling to stay warm in winter ever since there have been people—and winter. Cave people hovered round fires deep in caves. They wore extra furs. They even tied furs around their hands when they went hunting—the first gloves!

In Medieval times, people built fires in huge fireplaces. At night, they warmed their beds with hot bricks. They hung heavy curtains around their beds to keep in the warmth and keep out the drafts. Some wealthy people actually had servants lie down first and warm up their beds for them.

Nowadays, most of us have houses with thick walls and heaters. When we go outside to the store or to school or to play, we wear plenty of hoods and scarves and long johns and gloves and woolen socks. And of course, we try to keep moving. The best way to keep warm is to keep moving. So if you're outside in the cold and you're not going anywhere and just standing still, jump up and down. At outdoor football games, those people jumping up and down in the stands aren't just excited—they are trying to keep warm.

And of course when all else fails there is always a nice, hot bowl of chicken soup.

February has 28 days

In **February,** some people are still out making snowforts, but other people are sick of snow. For the sick of snow, we suggest making an indoor fort. From tables and chairs and blankets, you can create your own cozy bear cave. Deep in your cave, far from the snow, you can curl up, do a jigsaw puzzle, read a book, plan your spring— hobbies for the human hibernator.

Featured Creatures

FISH WEARS BIFOCALS
The anableps, a tropical fish, has eyes divided into an upper and a lower part. The fish swims with its eyes partly out of the water, and uses the upper part to see things in the air, the lower part to see under water.

INSECTS PLEAD INNOCENT
In 1545, the winegrowers of St. Julien, France, complained to a lawyer that snout beetles were eating up their grapes. The beetles were taken to court, given lawyers, and tried and convicted. They left town before punishment.

BEWARE OF GEESE!
The Romans claimed it was geese that saved the city from invaders in 338 B.C. They cackled so loudly they woke up the citizens who were able to fight off the enemy. Geese are still used as watchdogs today.

Skip Snaith

Symbols

February's flower is the **violet,** spring-blooming and often found growing wild. The birthstone—lavender to purple—is

amethyst, a gem that stands for sincerity.

Pisces

the fishes
Feb. 19 - March 21 

People born in Pisces are blessed with a keen intelligence and an active imagination. They are honest, sensitive, fond of beauty in Nature and Art; fond, too, of food. It is hard to ruffle Pisces for they are even-tempered and easy-going. Pisces are natural lovers.*

Famous people born in Pisces:
Enrico Caruso, operatic tenor, born 1873.
George Harrison, Beatle, born 1943.
Marian Anderson, opera contralto, born 1902.

Friends' birthdays:

* Remember to swallow with grain of salt, when necessary.

Ken Marcus Daly

February Past

Boy Scouting Begins
In February 1908, Sir Robert Baden-Powell founded an organization for boys 11 years and older. The Boy Scouts is intended to teach boys about the out-of-doors and to help them build strong minds and bodies.

Weather Watch Starts
The United States Weather Bureau started in 1870.

G.W. Visits Dismal Swamp
In February of 1763, George Washington, a member of the Draining Commission, paid a visit to Dismal Swamp, a 20-mile long, virtually impenetrable swamp located in southeast Virginia.

Holidays

Groundhog Day—February 2
St. Valentine's Day—February 14
Susan B. Anthony Day—February 15
Lincoln's Birthday—February 20
Leap Year Day—February 29 (every four years)
Chinese New Year—Sometime between January 21 and February 19

And

USE THIS SPACE TO WRITE IN YOUR FAVORITE FEBRUARY DAYS.

Saint Valentine's Day is the holiday for people in love—and that means practically everybody. The symbol for Valentine's Day is the valentine heart. If you look closely at it, you will see that actually it is a very neat way to make the human heart, for it is the human heart that is said to rule in love. On Valentine's Day, people send heart-shaped cards, lockets, boxes of candy and arrangements of flowers. The first valentine message was sent in February 1415, by the Duke of Orleans, from his cell in the Tower of London to his beloved wife at home. The idea of sending a sweet message caught on and lovers all over England soon were sending each other little poems every February. The first store to sell valentines opened in London in 1809. By the 1840's, valentines had gotten quite fancy: silk, satin, lacy, perfumed, musical, mechanical, bejeweled and stuffed. There are two main types of valentine cards: serious and silly, or lovey-dovey and "vinegar." Serious or silly, the valentine message always comes through sweet and clear: "I love you."

March has 31 days

March is a month of tricky winds. Some mornings, the balmy breeze makes you feel as if spring has come to stay. But don't you believe it and don't put away your muffler and mittens yet. Winter almost always comes back for a few more nasty, bitter swipes. And before the spring comes for good, March is a long, cold month.

EARTHQUAKES

The entire earth is covered with cracks called faults. Earthquakes happen when the rocks along the fault shift and slip. Earthquakes may not be very pleasant to those of us who like a nice, steady surface to walk on, but earthquakes do perform a necessary function. More than 1,200 recording stations around the world pick up 500,000 earthquake tremors a year. Earthquakes give the earth a facelift. With mountains wearing down, or eroding, if the earth weren't raised again, the world would be a place of stagnant seas.

When tremors occur in the earth beneath the ocean, waves called tsunami happen. Tsunami—or tidal waves—are walls of water over 200 feet high. Surf's up!

Symbols

The flower for March is

daffodil, yellow and trumpet-shaped.

The stone for March is **aquamarine.** It stands for truthfulness.

Aries

the ram
March 21 - April 20 

People born under the sign of Aries are booksmart and excellent at bossing others around. Stubbornness and inventiveness rule the Aries character. Friendly advice from an Aries is good advice. A typical Aries has a tendency to be overly concerned with neatness and stylishness.*

Famous people born in Aries:

Hans Christian Anderson, writer of fairy-tales, born 1805.

Werner von Braun, rocket scientist, born 1912.

Elton John, popular singer, born 1947.

Friends' birthdays:

* Remember to swallow with grain of salt, when necessary.

Ken Marcus Daly

March Past

Girl Scouting Underway

Mrs. Juliette Gordon Low, a Girl Guide leader in England, came to America and started the Girl Scouts in 1912. Like Girl Guides, it taught young girls seven to 17, crafts and outdoor skills.

Caesar Ignores Seer

Julius Caesar was slain by Marc Antony, Brutus and other members of the Roman Senate in March, 44 B.C. A seer had warned Caesar: "Beware the Ides of March." The seer was right.

Patrick Drums out Snakes

On March 17, 450 A.D., by beating on a drum, Patrick drove a plague of snakes out of Ireland.

Holidays

St. Patrick's Day—March 17
Bird Day (in Iowa)—March 21
Emancipation Day (in Puerto Rico)—March 22
Kuhio Day (in Hawaii)—March 26

And

USE THIS SPACE TO WRITE IN YOUR FAVORITE MARCH DAYS.

INCREDIBLE BUT TRUE

In TOPEKA, it is illegal for a waiter to serve WINE in a TEA CUP.

During wartime, a New York court ruled that "the defendant will be restrained from selling pickles but not from serving them with meals as a substitute for butter."

In Corvallis, Oregon, young women are not allowed to drink coffee after six o'clock in the evening.

California ordinance states babies may not be given coffee to drink.

IT IS AGAINST THE LAW FOR NEBRASKA TAVERN OWNERS TO SELL BEER UNLESS THEY HAVE A KETTLE FOR SOUP BREWING.

A citizen may not carry a **LUNCH PAIL** on the public streets of Riverside, California.

CREAM PUFFS were once declared against the pure drug and food law in Marion, Ohio.

IN OKLAHOMA, YOU CANNOT TAKE A BITE OF ANOTHER PERSON'S HAMBURGER.

THE ZODIAC

Aquarius—rules the legs
an airy sign
Good for making friends.
Good for doing business.
Good for getting rid of
pests.
Good for making sport.

Pisces—rules the feet
a watery sign
Good for marking hogs.
Good for pruning trees.
Good for weaning babies.

Aries—rules the head
a hot, dry sign
Good for planting beets.
Good for putting up
preserves.
Good for hunting.
Good for getting a
permanent hair wave.

Taurus—rules the neck
an airy sign
Good for planting all root
plants
Good for going to sales.
Good for going fishing.
Good for making pickles.

Gemini—rules the arms
an airy sign
Good for talking politics.
Good for discussing
things with friends.
Good for calling in the
exterminator.

Cancer—rules the breast
a watery sign
Best for planting flowers.
Good for planting grass
and clover.
Good for going to the
dentist.
Good for changing jobs.
Good for cutting hair.

ZODIAC
Leo—rules the heart
a fiery sign
No good for planting
anything.
Good for baking cakes.
Good for frollicking and
having fun.
Virgo—rules the bowels
an earth sign
No good for planting.
Good for doing business.
Libra—rules the kidneys
an airy sign
Good for planting above-
ground crops.
Good for making friends.
Good for doing business.
Scorpio—rules the loins
a watery sign
Best for above-ground
crops.
Best for flowers.
Best for fishing and
hunting.
Sagittarius—rules the
thighs
a fiery sign
Good for planting onions.
Good for planning
future.
Good for making candy.
Don't transplant.
Capricorn—rules the
knees
an earth sign
Best for planting all roots.
Good for pulling teeth.
Good for canning.

BIRTHDAY CAKES

Today, almost everybody who wants one gets a birthday party. Everybody gets a birthday cake. But this was not always so. Once, birthday parties were the special privilege of gods, spirits and noble people. In ancient China, people celebrated the birthday of the spirit of the harvest moon. They steamed cakes of yellow flour, molded in the shape of the full moon. The ancient Greeks, too, kept holidays for the moon, for the goddess of the moon, Artemis. Her birthday came once a month, 12 times a year. On her 12 special days, the Greeks baked yellow honey cakes in which they set long, thin candles. Before they blew out the candles and ate the cakes, they asked silent favors of the goddess. The Pharaoh's birthday party was the biggest event of the Egyptian year. On this day, slave and master sat down together to feast and make merry. In the 1600's people first began to celebrate the birthday of Christ, on Christmas, secretly at first, for the church did not approve. It approved even less that people were beginning to believe that the birthdays of ordinary, everyday folk were just as special and just as much worth remembering as those of gods and nobles. For the first time, parents began to record the dates on which their children were born, and to hold birthday parties every year. The Scandinavian birthday child got a kringle, a cake shaped like a pretzel, topped with sugar and raisins and almonds. The German child requested a favorite dish for birthday supper. Parents lit a candle for the birthday child in the morning and let it burn the day long, to ensure a long and happy life. On the frosted birthday cake were as many candles as the child was old. All the children together wished on the candles and blew them out. If all the candles went out, each wish would come true. If the flames sputtered, surprises were in store. In America, the birthday child, alone, blows out the candles. With one candle added for every year, the older a child gets, the harder it is to blow out those candles and make that wish come true.

Spring

When the sun strikes the earth further and further north, toward the Tropic of Cancer, north of the equator by 23½ degrees, it is spring here in the northern half of the world, while it is autumn in the southern half. Spring is the windiest of seasons. If the calendar didn't let you know on March 21, you would still know that it is spring. One day, you can't seem to keep your mind on school work. You are first restless, then sluggish. You find yourself daydreaming, staring out the window. You feel as if something wonderful were about to happen. You are on the edge of your seat. Yes, along with the first robin and the first crocus, spring fever is a sure sign that spring is in the wind. As dogs and cats shed their shaggy winter coats, you shed your winter coat. The spring showers fall. The trees bud. The forsythia blooms. The daffodils appear. The birds return. Day by day, the spring comes in.

Winds

In this, the windiest of seasons, the winds range from light breeze to gale. Here is a way you can tell how fast the wind is blowing just by looking at the effect it has on a single tree:

4 - 6 miles per hour	light breeze	leaves rustle
11-16 miles per hour	moderate breeze	small branches move
22-27 miles per hour	strong breeze	large branches sway
28-33 miles per hour	moderate gale	whole tree sways
48-55 miles per hour	full gale	branches may snap
64-71 miles per hour	hurricane	whole tree may blow away

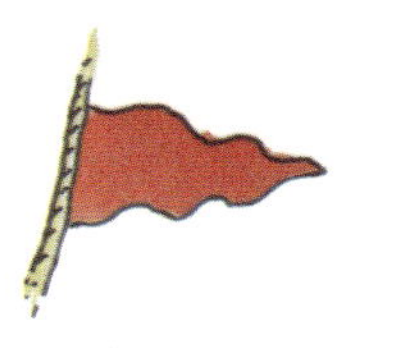

Small Craft

N.E. Storm

S.E. Storm

S.W. Storm

N.W. Storm

Hurricane or Whole Gale

April has 30 days

April is a month famous for its showers. There is no better way to ease spring fever than to don slicker and rubbers and splash through the puddles, squish through the mud. On farms, people are busy planting. You, too, can put in your garden. And if you don't care to wait for the autumn harvest, here is an excellent way to sprout a crop in just a few days.

Sproutíng

You can sprout almost any grain, bean or seed. The tastiest things to sprout are soybeans, alfalfa, lentils, peas, oats and wheat.

First, wash the seeds and pick out any seeds that float. Floating seeds are sterile and they will never sprout. Put a tablespoon or two or three in a clean pint jar (see fig. 1). Soak overnight in three times as much water in a warm, dark place (see fig. 2). Be sure and use bottled water, as chlorine tends to sterilize the seeds.

Next morning, pour off the water. The seeds should be swollen to twice their size. Leave the seeds in the jar, cover with cheese cloth or strainer and place at a 45 degree angle back in that warm, dark place (see fig. 4).

Twice every day, flush the seeds with fresh water. In three to six days, depending on the temperature and the seed, you will have sprouted seeds.

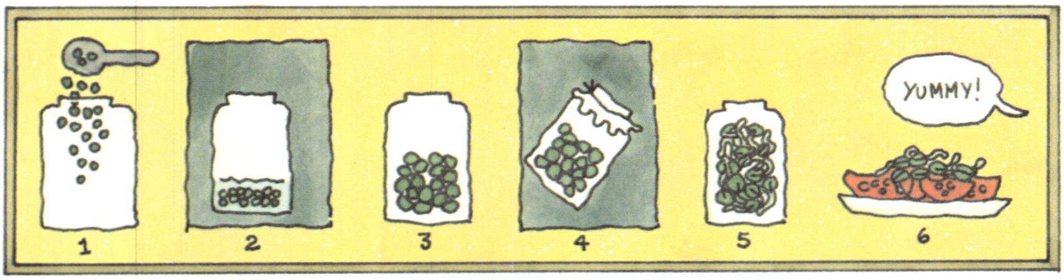

Sprouts are tasty and full of vitamins. Try them plain or with salad dressing. Sprinkle them over your vegetables. Put them in your sandwiches. How about sprouts with spaghetti sauce?

Symbols

The flower for April is the sweet-smelling climber, **sweet pea,** which blooms white to deep red and purple.

Diamond is the birthstone. It stands for innocence.

Taurus

the bull
April 20 - May 21 

People born under the sign of Taurus are natural leaders. They are strong-willed and demanding of those who serve them, yet sympathetic at the same time. They appreciate the finer things in life, especially fine books. Beware of stubbornness, Taureans!*

Famous people born in Taurus:
Ella Fitzgerald, jazz singer, born 1918.
Catherine the Great, empress of all the Russias, 1792.
Florence Nightingale, reformer of nurses' training, born 1820.

Friends' birthdays:

*Remember to swallow with grain of salt, when necessary.

Ken Marcus Daly

April Past

The Mail Must Gallop Through

In April 1860, the first Pony Express rider carried mail from St. Joseph, Missouri to Sacramento, California, galloping at top speed and changing horses every 15 miles.

G.W. Takes Oath

On April 30, 1789, after a triumphal journey from his Mt. Vernon estate, Washington stood on the balcony of Federal Hall in New York City and took the first oath of office of the Presidency of the United States.

American Civil War Begins, April 1861.
American Revolution Begins, April 1775.
Spanish American War Begins, April 1898.

Holidays

April Fool's Day—April 1
Good Friday—the Friday before Easter Sunday
Arbor Day—date varies from state to state

And

USE THIS SPACE TO WRITE IN YOUR FAVORITE APRIL DAYS.

April is a giddy month, a month of spring fever and restlessness. And isn't April the month when all people are nature's fools? One day, it is bright and sunny. The next day, it is raining pitchforks. And some days, it rains and shines at the same time! So it isn't at all surprising that April is the month when the practical joke gets a holiday all its own.

April Fool's Day is thought by many people to be the most insignificant of all holidays. The only way in which it has changed the course of history is that it has given rise to the novelty and practical joke business. Laugh boxes, squirting flowers, fake flies in plastic ice cubes, air cushions and plastic puke are just a few of the gizmoes people buy and use to play practical jokes on one another come April first. Some of the best practical jokes are those you make up yourself. Next April first, at the breakfast table, try telling sleepy Dad he has egg on the tip of his nose. Watch the expression on his face. Or why not send your little brother or sister on an errand to the store for some freeze dried ostrich eggs?

Since the first cave person dressed up in a bearskin and came growling after his neighbor (hopefully unarmed at the time), people have enjoyed playing harmless practical jokes on one another. Throughout history, there have been holidays set aside for silliness. The Indians still have a holiday on which they trick each other into running useless or "sleeveless" errands. The ancient Romans celebrated Hilaria, a festival to the goddess of spring. The first April Fool's Day, as we know it, probably happened in France in the 1500's when the Gregorian calendar was used for the first time. The Gregorian calendar moved New Years' Day from the end of March to the first of January. In April, people with a sense of humor paid visits to their more serious and forgetful friends, bearing New Year's gifts and greetings. "Happy New Year!" was the call of the first April Fooler.

To throw your custard pie, follow these easy instructions:
Locate likely victim.
Hold pie in palm, behind back.
Lift pie and throw in face of victim.
Smear pie to cover edges of face, nose, hair, neck, etc.

BEFORE DURING AFTER

CHEAP LAUGHS HAHA

April Fool!

May has 31 days

'Tis the month of **May** and the world is in flower. And it is with flowers that people since prehistoric times have been celebrating or "bringing in" the May. Make crowns and bracelets of dandelions and wildflowers. Pick your favorite tree to be your Maypole. Dance around the Maypole and rejoice, for spring is here and winter won't be back until you are good and ready for it.

Wonderful Worms

Earthworms are largely responsible for bringing in the May. They may not be nearly as pretty as flowers, but they are some of nature's most helpful creatures. Earthworms are happiest in the earth, where it is dark and damp. They do not like sunlight and they do not like dryness. A warm, dry earthworm is a dead one. They don't like being flooded, either, and that is why you see so many earthworms wriggling on the garden path after a rainstorm. Earthworms live in burrows beneath gardens and lawns. They dig their burrows by eating the earth and digesting it as they crawl. Often as deep as eight feet beneath the earth, these burrows bring air to the roots of plants, aiding their growth. Each time an earthworm digests, it fertilizes the earth with rich earthworm manure. It fertilizes as it plows. One small earthworm won't fertilize an entire garden, but thousands of earthworms can make the difference between a sickly garden and a healthy one. The common enemies of the earthworm are the robin, the mole, the centipede, the platypus and the person who likes to fish.

Symbols

The flower for the month of May is the **lily of the valley,** a dainty white, bell-shaped blossom that grows in shade. The birthstone is **emerald,** symbol of happiness.

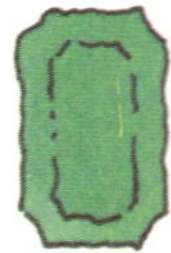

Gemini

the twins
May 21 - June 21 ♊

People born under the sign of Gemini have sunny dispositions. They are often the life of the party and make excellent hosts and hostesses. Gemini are skilled with their hands and very good teachers. They should avoid letting small problems send them into tantrums.*

Famous people born in Gemini:
Queen Victoria of England, born 1819.
John Fitzgerald Kennedy, born 1917.
Harriet Beecher Stowe, author, born 1811.
Socrates, philosopher, born 469 B.C.

Friends' birthdays:

*Remember to swallow with grain of salt, when necessary.

Ken Marcus Daly

May Past

Lusitania Sinks

In May 1915, German U-boats—submarines—torpedoed and sank the *Lusitania,* a passenger ship carrying over 2,000 people.

Hindenberg Explodes

In May 1937, on its way from Germany, the dirigible, *Hindenberg,* blew up in mid-air over New Jersey.

"Lucky Lindy"

On a rainy morning in May 1927, a former airmail pilot took off from Long Island, New York in his single-engine airplane *The Spirit of St. Louis.* Thirty-three-and-one-half hours later, he landed safely in Paris. It was the first solo flight over the Atlantic.

Holidays

May Day—May 1
Rhode Island Independence Day—May 4
Easter Sunday—On the Sunday following the first full moon after the spring equinox, sometime between March 22 and April 25.
Mother's Day—second Sunday in May
Memorial Day—May 30

And

USE THIS SPACE TO WRITE IN YOUR FAVORITE MAY DAYS.

COMMON WILDFLOWERS

Chicory
cichorium itybus

Yarrow
achillea millefolium

Pokeweed
phytolacca americana

Violet
viola pedata

Field Mustard
brassica arvensis

Pearly Everlasting
anaphalis margaritacea

Linda Snaith

June has 30 days

June is the school-is-out month and there are more hours in the day than you know what to do with. June is a fine month in which to run around and play. It's not too hot and not too cool. It's just right for flying a kite, throwing a ball, swinging a racket. June is a just-right time for some people to get married.

Wedding Lore

The crude cartoon of the caveman dragging off the cavewoman by the hair may be ridiculous but it is not altogether historically incorrect. The original marriage was marriage by capture. When a man wanted to get married, he assembled his best friends and, together, they captured his bride. The friends fought off the bride's family, while the groom snatched her from the hut and ran off with her in his arms, as she kicked and screamed. Often the bride had to be tied up for days until she settled down and got used to the idea of being a married woman.

Today, weddings are more pleasant occasions. But there remain three signs of the bad old days of marriage by capture. The best friend or "best man" is still on hand to help the groom. The wedding ring symbolizes the rope with which the bride sometimes was bound. And the groom still carries the bride over the threshold.

Skip Snaith

Symbols

June's flower is the **rose** which has grown wild since prehistoric times.

The birthstone for June is **moonstone,** which stands for health and long life.

Cancer

the crab
June 21 - July 23 

People born under the sign of Cancer are dependable, affectionate, and motherly. Since the talents of crabs are many, they should avoid trying to do too many things at once. Crabs are known to store away their money. They are fond of babies, of travel, and of daydreaming.*

Famous people born in Cancer:

Helen Keller, author and lecturer, blind and deaf from age two, born 1880.

Phineas Taylor Barnum, showman, circus-founder, born 1810.

Friends' birthdays:

* Remember to swallow with grain of salt, when necessary.

Ken Marcus Daly

June Past

Napoleon Loses

In June 1815, at the Battle of Waterloo, Napoleon I suffered his final defeat at the hands of the British and allies.

Magna Carta Signed

In June 1215, King John of England was forced by his barons to sign the Magna Carta. The Magna Carta limited forever the king's power in England. Ever since, no king of England has taken the name John.

Secret Service Now in Service

In June 1860, the first United States Secret Service was started under President Lincoln. The service people protected the president and spied.

Holidays

Kamehameha Day (in Hawaii)—June 11
Flag Day—June 14
Father's Day—third Sunday in June

And

USE THIS SPACE TO WRITE IN YOUR FAVORITE JUNE DAYS.

GO FLY A KITE

MAKE NOTCHES IN ENDS & PUT STRING AROUND THE EDGE (TIE OR GLUE IT)

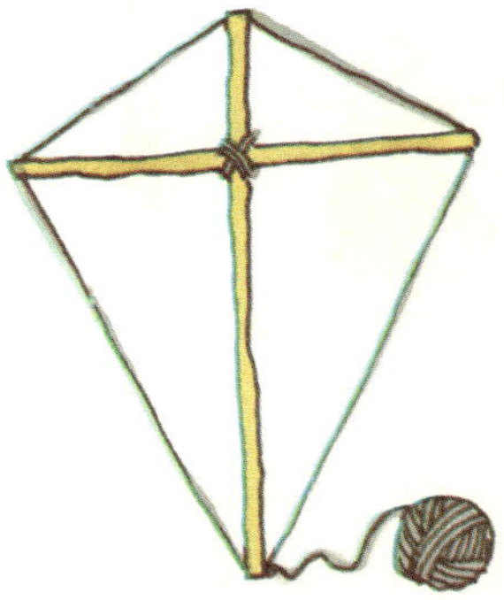

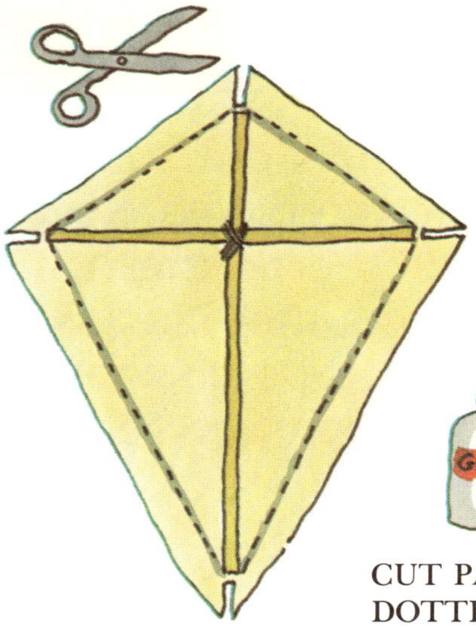

TWO PIECES OF BALSA WOOD

NO NOTCH

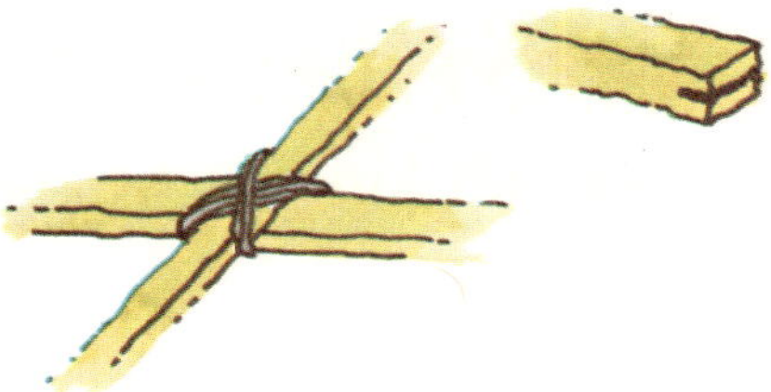

LASH JOINT WITH STRING

CUT

CUT

FOLD & GLUE

CUT

CUT PATTERN & FOLD ON DOTTED LINE (YOU CAN USE NEWSPAPER OR BROWN WRAPPING PAPER)

COVER SHOULD BE A LITTLE LOOSE & FLAPPY

ADD STRING & TAIL

PAINT YOUR KITE. HERE ARE SOME IDEAS

HEAVY WEATHER

TORNADO

A tornado is a rotating storm, consisting of a violent, swiftly moving column of air. A tornado looks like a dark funnel and sounds like a roaring locomotive. Defense: Go to basement or tornado cellar until it has passed.

HURRICANE

A hurricane is a wind storm that starts in tropical ocean waters and moves clockwise toward the northern hemisphere and counter-clockwise toward the southern hemisphere. Defense: Bring in boat; go to basement.

FLOOD

A flood happens when water overflows its natural confines, usually during spring thaw. Floods are the biggest problem in low-lying geographical areas. Defense: Go to attic or highest point on property. If you climb a tree, make sure it's a tall one.

SELF-DEFENSE

DROUGHT

A drought is a condition caused when no rain has fallen for a long time. Droughts result in dried up river and stream beds, dried up soil and plant-life. Defense: irrigation. Don't eat popcorn or other salty foods.

TYPHOON

A typhoon is a wind storm, just like a hurricane, except that it happens in the western Pacific. Typhoons are more severe than hurricanes because the wind has a wider stretch of ocean over which to build up. Defense: see hurricane.

BLIZZARD

A blizzard is a heavy snowstorm with high winds. Defense: During a blizzard, avoid going outside. After a blizzard, wear snowshoes and carry a shovel and a red flag, just in case you get stuck in a drift.

Weather Signs

It's going to rain when—
the leaves show their backs.
the cows lie down in the pasture.
the ants cover the tops of their hills.
the tips of the moon point down.

Rain

We're in for a dry spell when—
dogs and cats wallow in the dirt.
there's heavy dew in the mornings.
ants bring up their eggs to bake and hatch in the sun.

Dry

Fair

It will be fair when—
there are soft, fluffy clouds high in the sky.
the sunset the day before was clear.
the spiders are busy making webs.

Snow

It is going to snow when—
cats and dogs curl up with their noses in their tails.
the birds fly low.

Summer

When the sun strikes the earth along the Tropic of Cancer, 23½ degrees north of the equator, it is summer in the northern half of the world, while it is winter in the southern half. Summer is a word that comes from the Sanskrit word *sama,* meaning "half year." We only wish it lasted half the year. If the calendar didn't tell you so on June 21, you would still know that it is summer. The days are long and hot. At the night, the lightning bugs are out, the bushes full of crickets. During the day, dogs pant and dig cool beds in the dust. The azelia, the lilac, and the rhododendron have withered and gone for the year. The tiger lily, the honeysuckle and the rose are in bloom. It is warm enough to swim. It sometimes is so warm you wish you were lying in a large bowl of lemonade. You spend long hours lying on your back, staying cool and taking it easy. While you are lying on your back this summer, staying cool and taking it easy, try a little cloud watching.

Watching CLOUDS

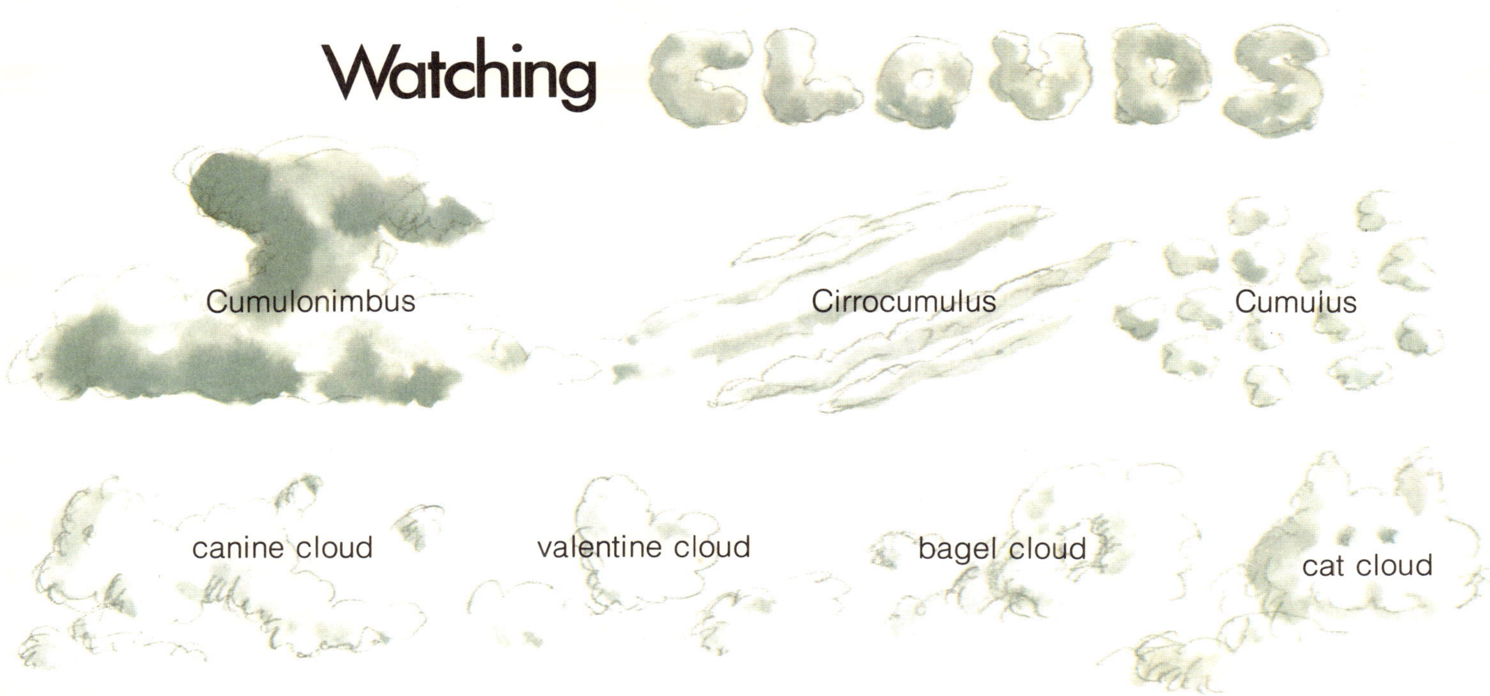

There are two main types of cloud: cumulus and stratus. Cumulus clouds are puffy and piled up. Stratus are layered or in sheets. For maximum cloud watching pleasure, pick a day having cumulus clouds. Cumulus cloud-watching is more interesting than stratus cloud-watching. Who wants to watch a low, leaden sky? Cirrus clouds are high and wispy. Cumulonimbus, or thunderheads, are flat on the bottom and piled high. Cirrocumulus clouds sometimes form in bands or in puffs. Like cracks in a ceiling, if you look at them with a little imagination, clouds turn into other things: castles, mare's tails, freshly plowed fields. And unlike a ceiling, the sky is forever changing, moving, and forming new pictures.

July has 31 days

July is the month during which it is important to stay cool. You can run a lemonade stand, or stand under a sprinkler, or splash in a pool. You can sleep without blankets, or in a tent in the back yard. Kitchens are especially hot, so people cook outdoors in July. While you enjoy the barbecue, you can count the lightning bugs. And speaking of lightning. . . .

ELECTRICAL STORMS

The sky on the horizon is slate gray. A blast of cold air hits you in the face. You hear thunder in the distance, and you head for the house. Yes, a thunderstorm is on the way. A good way to avoid getting the jitters as the storm comes closer and closer, is to judge the distance of the thunderstorm from your home. Here's how: Light travels at about 186,000 miles per second. Sound travels at 1,100 feet per second. This means that sound travels about one mile in five seconds. To judge how far from you a thunderstorm is, you time how long it takes the sound of thunder to reach you, after the lightning has flashed. By counting, "1,001—1,002—1,003—1,004," and so on, at a normal rate, you can count seconds. Using this system, if you can count from 1,001 to 1,010 from the time you see the lightning until the time you hear the thunder, you know that the thunderstorm is about two miles away from you.

Symbols

Water lily is July's flower, which floats on ponds and pools on rounded leaves.

The birthstone for July is **ruby.** Ruby means contentment.

Leo

the lion
July 23 - August 23 ♌

People born under the sign of Leo possess strong will and strong, noble character, traits which make Leos natural leaders. They tend to be moody and need to be reminded to cheer up. Leos enjoy studying and their hobbies are of an intellectual and cultured nature.*

Famous people born in Leo:
Amelia Earhart, first woman to solo fly Atlantic, born 1898.
Henry VIII of England, known for his eight wives, born 1457.
Davy Crockett, frontiersperson, born 1786.

Friends' birthdays:

* Remember to swallow with grain of salt, when necessary.

Ken Marcus Daly

July Past

People on Moon
On July 16, 1969, at 9:32 A.M., Earth Time, Astronaut Neil Armstrong stepped out of the Apollo II, onto the surface of the moon.

First World's Fair Opens
On July 14, 1853, the first World's Fair Exhibition opened in New York's Flushing Meadow.

Salvation Army Forms
In July 1865, the Salvation Army was started in London, by William Booth, in order to do good social works and to help the needy.

Holidays

Independence Day—July 4
Bastille Day (in France)—July 14
Pioneer Day (in Utah)—July 14

And

USE THIS SPACE TO WRITE IN YOUR FAVORITE JULY DAYS.

Independence Day

Ever since the Continental Congress gathered in Philadelphia in July 1776 to adopt the Declaration of Independence, Americans have gone all out to celebrate the anniversary of the founding of the nation. The first such celebration occured just one year after that fateful date. On July 4, 1777, bells rang, cannon boomed, bonfires and fireworks flared, soldiers and revelers marched through the streets of Philadelphia, New York and Boston. Phila-

delphians placed lit candles in their windows. In fact, patriotic ruffians threw stones through the windows without candles. On July 4, 1788, Philadelphians organized a Fourth of July celebration that was to set the standard for all Fourths to come. Citizens who did not march, thronged the streets to watch a most spectacular parade. Heading up the procession was a carriage in the shape of the American eagle, bearing the Chief Justice of the Supreme Court.

Ten men walked by its side, arms linked, symbolizing the ten states that ratified the Constitution. Next came a float in the shape of the Federal Building. Most impressive of all was the military ship, *Union,* set on a float and mounted with 20 guns. The parade wound up at Bush Hill, where a lengthy ovation was given and a 20-gun salute. Then, practically all of Philadelphia sat down to picnic. There were cheeses as big around as wagon wheels, giant loaves of bread, whole barbecued oxen, tubs of anniversary punch. Word of

this grand celebration spread and, in the Fourths to follow, towns and cities across the nation would compete to see which could come up with the most dazzling display of patriotism. As the nation expanded westward, settlers carried with them the custom of celebrating the Fourth of July with parades, picnics, ovations, fireworks, and proud remembrances of the day when a tiny group of colonies made its stand against the Crown of Britain—and won independence.

August has 31 days

August is a good time for summer reading, in a hammock or in the crook of a shady tree. It is a fine time for collecting seashells and pinecones and other bits of nature. It is a perfect time for picking tomatoes (they should be ripe by now). A ripe tomato, fresh from the vine, is tastier than a slice of pizza. And speaking of pizza, did you know that garlic is good for you?

GARLIC SAVES

For over 5,000 years, folk doctors have prescribed the eating or rubbing on of garlic to cure or relieve such ailments as hysteria, hoarseness, worms, high blood pressure, headaches, colds, fever, indigestion, gout, pimples and The Plague. The Egyptian slaves who built the pyramid at Cheops were given daily doses of garlic to keep up their strength. The Vikings filled the holds of their ships with garlic. Today, in Bulgaria, where people live to be an active 100 and over, they chew garlic like gum. In Russia, a common remedy for the cold is to place pieces of garlic on either side of the mouth between cheek and teeth. In hours, the cold will disappear. So will all friends. Garlic may shoo away germs, but it also will shoo away most people. Garlic is so powerful that if you rub your feet with it (to cure bunions, of course), it will give you garlic breath!

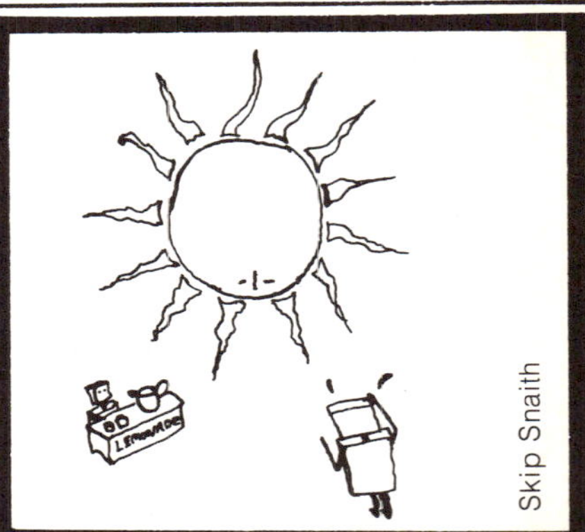

Symbols

August's flower is the **gladiolus,** which grows in Africa.

The birthstone is **peridot,** a gem that stands

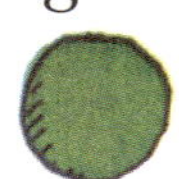

for happiness.

Virgo

the virgin
August 23 - Sept. 23 ♍

People born under the sign of Virgo have high ideals and short patience with ignorance. They are loyal to friends and are most particular about the friends that they choose. Virgoans catch on quickly to instructions, welcome puzzles and problems, may be scholarly types.*

Famous people born in Virgo:
Alexander the Great, born 35 B.C.
Letitzia Bonaparte, mother of Napoleon, born 1750.
Confucius, ancient Chinese teacher of ethics, born 551 B.C.

Friends' birthdays:

* Remember to swallow with grain of salt, when necessary.

Ken Marcus Daly

August Past

Columbus Sets Sail

In August 1492, Christopher Columbus set sail from Spain with 93 sailors in three small ships—the *Nina,* the *Pinta* and the *Santa Maria.*

Women Vote

In August 1920, an Amendment to the Constitution passed three quarters of the House. It said: "The right of citizens of the United States to vote shall not be denied . . . on account of sex."

No Folly for Fulton

Robert Fulton made the first steamboat trip on the *Clermont,* up the Hudson from New York City to Albany, on August 17.

Holidays

Friendship Day—August 2
Ernie Pyle Day (in New Mexico)—August 3
Huey P. Long's Birthday (in Louisiana)—August 30

And

USE THIS SPACE TO WRITE IN YOUR FAVORITE AUGUST DAYS.

DUNE GRASS
AT THE SEASHORE
DRIFTWOOD
SEAGULL
LITTER
CRAB
CLAM SHELLS
SMALL TIDEPOOL
SCALLOP SHELL
HORSESHOE CRAB
STARFISH
SNAIL
FISH
Linda Snaith

September has 30 days

September is here.
September is back-to-school month. It is a new month. A time for new clothes, new shoes, new books, new pencil boxes, new classmates and new teachers. It is sometimes hard to love September when you have to go back to school, but many people find September the most beautiful month of all. The corn is ripe and the leaves are turning. The world is blue and gold and fiery red.

Why go to School?

As another fabulous summer draws to a close, what youngster doesn't grumble, "Aw, gee, why do we have to go to school?" The answer, of course, is to learn things. There have always been things to learn. Cave children probably had to learn to hunt and skin wild animals, to gather nuts and berries. When life became more complicated, so did the things children had to learn, and so schools were started. The first schools were in ancient Greece. The word "school" comes from the Greek word meaning "leisure." This is not because school was a leisurely way to spend the day, but because only the leisure classes—or very wealthy people—could afford to send their children. It was not until the past two hundred years that schools opened their doors to all children. So remember, the next time you take to grumbling, that it was not so long ago when going to school was a rare and special privilege. And when you stop to think about it—all the fine things that you learn and friends that you meet—it still is.

Skip Snaith

Symbols

September's flower is the **morning glory,** with funnel-shaped blossoms that open in the morning.

The birthstone this month is **sapphire.** Sapphire stands for wisdom.

Libra

scales of balance
Sept. 23 - Oct. 23

People born under the sign of Libra are famous lovers of the out-of-doors. They are handsome and graceful, lovers of peace and quiet. Librans like nothing better than to relax and take it easy. Learn to budget your money, you Librans!*

Famous people born in Libra:
Sarah Bernhardt, French actress, born 1844.
Noah Webster, compiler of *The American Dictionary of the English Language,* born 1758.
Eleanor Roosevelt, born 1884.

Friends' birthdays:

* Remember to swallow with grain of salt, when necessary.

Ken Marcus Daly

September Past

Howe Sews Up Patent
Elias Howe patented his invention, the first mechanical sewing machine, in September of 1846.

"Oh say can you see?"
The British had been firing on the Americans in Fort McHenry all through the September night. When American lawyer, Francis Scott Key saw that the American flag still flew over the fort in the morning, he was inspired to write the immortal *Star Spangled Banner.*

London Burns
In September 1666, a huge fire destroyed most of London, which was later largely rebuilt by Sir Christopher Wren.

Holidays

Labor Day—September 2
General von Steuben Memorial Day—September 17

And

USE THIS SPACE TO WRITE IN YOUR FAVORITE SEPTEMBER DAYS.

Apples

The apple is the single most important fruit in the world. You will come across it wherever you look: in history, in legend and lore, in superstition, and last, but certainly not least, in kitchens and recipes all over the world. The first famous apple was that notorious piece of fruit that caused Adam and Eve to be thrown out of the Garden. Charred remains of apple were uncovered in ancient Swiss ruins. In Greek mythology, it was the apple, actually, and not Helen, that started the Trojan Wars. The so-called apple of discord was a golden apple inscribed to "the fairest." The Trojan prince, Paris had to decide which of three goddesses to present it to. Of Hera, Aphrodite, and Pallas Athena, he chose to give it to Aphrodite. In gratitude, Aphrodite gave him Helen. Helen's husband did not approve of the match. He started the Trojan Wars to win her home. In more recent times, no name is more apple-associated than John Chapman, otherwise known as Johnny Appleseed. He is the kindest and gentlest of all American folk heroes. So that the pioneers might have fresh fruit when they came West, Johnny Appleseed forged ahead into the American wilderness, barefooted, planting apple orchards throughout the Midwest as far as Indiana. Apples are useful, too. They clean teeth, for one. An apple after a meal is the perfect tooth-cleanser (and it's far tastier than toothpaste). Apples clean aluminum, for another. You can clean a tarnished aluminum pot by boiling water with apple peels in it. Apples keep bread fresh. Keep a section of apple in your bread bin and baked goods will stay moist. Superstitions connected with apples are equally ample. If you peel an apple in one long piece, count off the twists by the letters of the alphabet. The last letter will begin the name of your future sweetheart. To cut an apple in half without cutting the seeds brings good fortune. Other apple-isms are: apple of the eye, which means favorite; apples of Sodom, which means disappointment; apple polisher, which is one who tries overly hard to win a teacher's favor, and the Big Apple, which is New York City.

SUPERSTITIONS

It's bad luck to open an umbrella in the house. It's good luck to sneeze three times in a row. Break a mirror, seven years' bad luck. Most superstitions may not seem to make much sense. But behind most superstitions, lie logical explanations. For instance:

Drop a spoon, visitor soon.
People outside your door overhear and think you are fixing supper. They drop in on the chance they might get some.

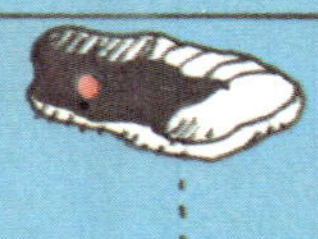

It's bad luck to keep slippers and shoes on the top shelf.
If they fall, you get hit on the head: right?

It's bad luck to make a dog look in the mirror.
Dogs tend to get irritated when you make them do anything.
For good luck ask them nicely.

It's bad luck to walk under a ladder.
A ladder usually means people are working.
People working means danger of falling buckets, brushes, workers, etc.

It's unlucky to put a hat on a bed.
Right: you might sit on it by mistake.

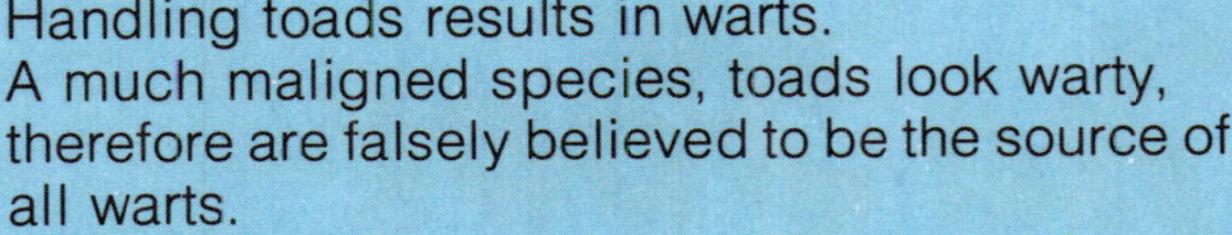

Handling toads results in warts.
A much maligned species, toads look warty, therefore are falsely believed to be the source of all warts.

It's bad luck when a black cat crosses your path.
Black cats are associated with witches. Black cat means witch nearby. Witches make people nervous. In their nervousness, people bring bad fortune on themselves.

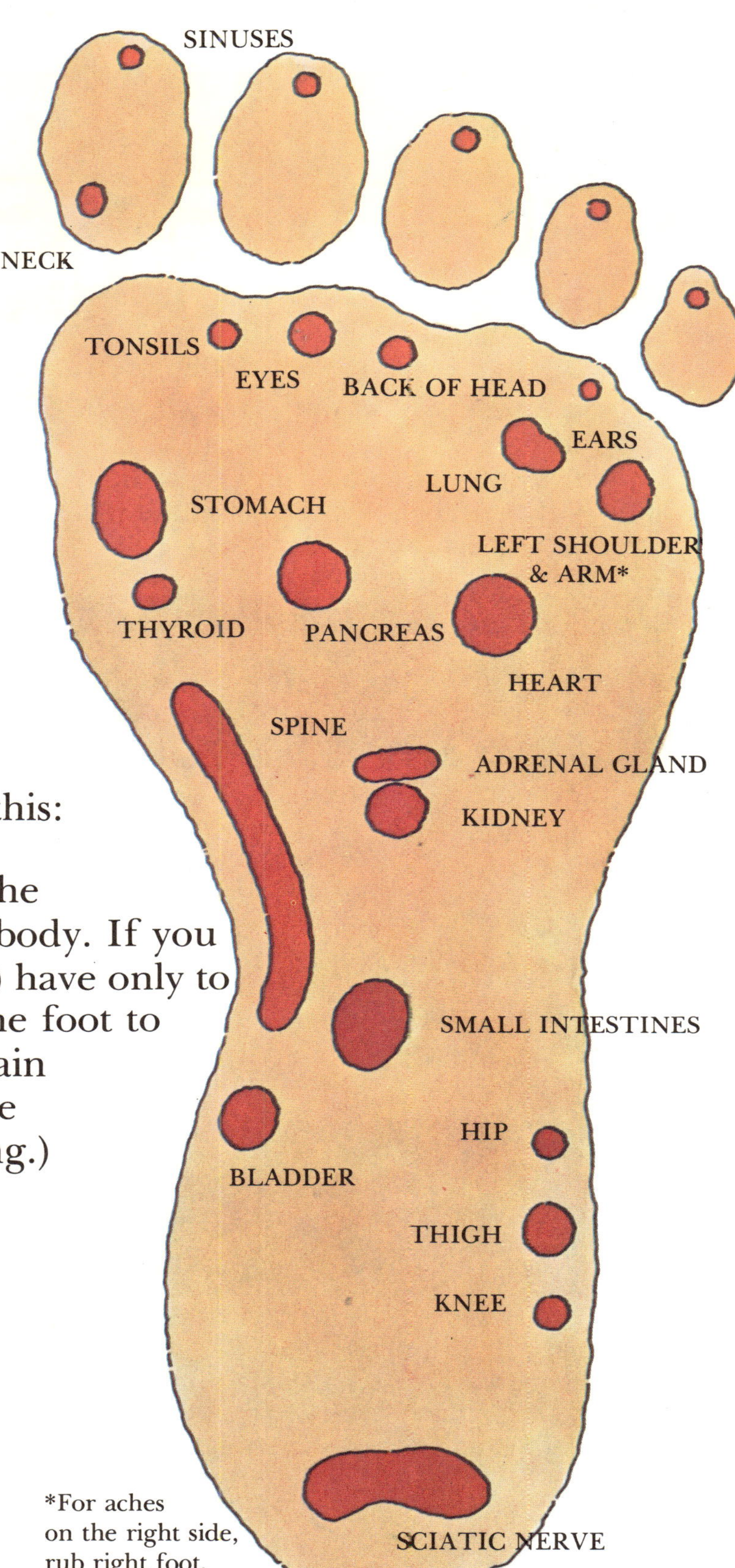

The latest fad from the Fix-It-Yourselfers is the Fantastic, New-fangled, Never-fail FOOT MASSAGE. It works like this:

Each part of the foot sole is connected, via the nervous system, to each major organ in the body. If you have an ache in your organ, you (or a friend) have only to rub the corresponding area on the sole of the foot to ease that ache. For instance, if you have a pain in the neck, simply rub your big toe until the pain goes away. (This may take some rubbing.) All this is fine and dandy. But what do you do if you have a pain in the foot? Which part of the foot corresponds to the foot?

The Foot

*For aches on the right side, rub right foot, same spot.

The Moon

People say in jest that the moon is made of green cheese, but many people actually used to believe it. There was even a time when they believed that there was a man in the moon in charge of the lantern of moonlight. And at another time, scientists thought the moon was covered with oceans full of serpents. Nowadays, people

know better. People know that the moon is a dead dry rock, 2,160 miles in diameter, revolving around the earth in a not-quite circular orbit every 27 days, 7 hours, 43 minutes, and that the moon rotates on its axis once during this time. It is known, too, that the moon doesn't really change its shape, it merely appears to change its shape as its position relative to the sun and earth shifts. After absence from the sky for a few nights, it appears as a light crescent in the far western sky. Night after night, it moves farther west, increasing to full moon. It remains full a few nights and then begins to decrease in size, once more becoming crescent-shaped. The moon as it becomes fuller is called waxing moon; as it becomes smaller, waning moon.

Many people believe that the moon causes more things to happen on earth than just the shifting of tides. Here are some of the strange beliefs connected with the moon. Read them. Try some of them. Judge for yourself whether or not they make sense. For the most comfortable feather bed, stuff it after the moon has passed full. It is bad luck to point at the full moon. When you see the new moon, bow seven times and jingle the change in your pocket for good luck. To sleep in the light of the full moon causes moon burn. To rid your house of spiders, clean it in the new moon. Hair and nails will remain short longer if you cut them in the waning moon. Medicines are more effective taken in the full moon.

Fall

When the sun strikes the earth further and further south, toward the Tropic of Capricorn, 23½ degrees south of the equator, it is autumn here in the northern half of the world, spring in the southern half. Autumn is the harvest season. If the calendar didn't tell you so on September 23, you would still know that it is autumn. The leaves are turning to burnt brown, fire red, pumpkin orange, moon yellow. The dogs and cats and squirrels have begun once more to grow their winter coats. Squirrels are busy storing up acorns and other nuts. Dogs bury their bones. Birds eat the berries. Apples grow heavy on the branch. Birds and butterflies head south. And people head back from their vacations, to school, to work, to harvest, and to feast.

THE AUTUMN LEAVES

October has 31 days

October is the month of the final harvest before the frost. October is the time for roasted chestnuts and pumpkin seeds. It is the time for raking leaves and jumping in them. October is an apple month—apple cider, apple sauce, roasted apple and bushel baskets of apples. The leaves are at their most colorful, before they turn gray and fall and crumble. The days are bright and blustery. The nights are windy and moody. October is a spooky, creepy, time of year.

JACK-O-LANTERNS

Irish legend tells how Stingy Jack trapped the Devil in an apple tree and would not set him free until the Devil promised never to claim his soul. But when Jack died, Heaven turned him away. And when he sought entrance to Hell, the Devil kicked him out and tossed a live coal after him. Jack, who happened to be snacking on a turnip at the time, put the coal in the turnip and ever after roamed the earth, glowing turnip for his lantern. On Halloween, Irish children remember Stingy Jack by carving faces in turnips and potatoes and placing lit candles inside. They call them Jack-o-lanterns. When Irish people brought Halloween with them to the United States in the 1840's, they began to use pumpkins instead. A pumpkin makes for better carving than a turnip or a potato. And pumpkin pie is far tastier than turnip pie. Can you imagine dressing up in a potato costume next Halloween? Or decorating your Halloween party table with black cats and grinning turnips?

Symbols

October's flower is **calendula,** also called marigold. It has a yellowish-gold head.

The birthstone for October is

opal. Opal means hope.

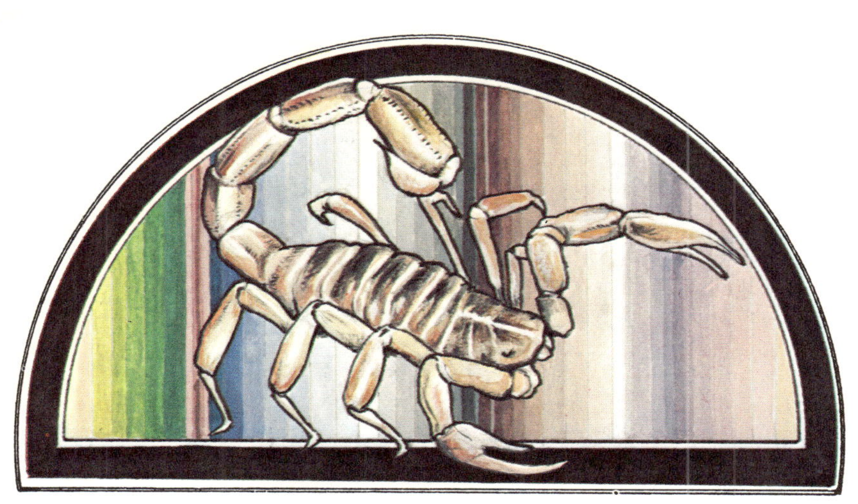

Scorpio

the scorpion
Oct. 23 - Nov. 22 

People born under the sign of Scorpio usually are excellent public speakers. They tire easily of routine and long for adventure, yet they have their sensible and practical sides, too. Praise and flattery is music to their ears.*

Famous people born in Scorpio:

Pablo Picasso, Spanish artist, born 1881.

Marie Antoinette, pleasure-loving queen of Louis XVI of France, born 1758.

Marie Curie, discoverer of radium, born 1867.

Friends' birthdays:

*Remember to swallow with grain of salt, when necessary.

Ken Marcus Daly

October Past

"T"—Time

In October 1908, Henry Ford built the first Model "T", later produced in large quantities on an assembly line. The Model "T" came in black only.

"Land!"

On October 11, 1492, Columbus spotted the first land of the New World and landed on what is now called Watling's Island. He thought it was Asia.

"Crash!"

The Great American Depression began when the stock market collapsed in October of 1929.

Holidays

Columbus Day—October 12
Poetry Day—October 15
Child Health Day—first Monday in October
Halloween—October 31

And

USE THIS SPACE TO WRITE IN YOUR FAVORITE OCTOBER DAYS.

Witches are old and nasty and ugly as all get-out. Everybody who has ever read a fairy tale or gone trick-or-treating knows that. Witches have long warty chins that reach up to touch their long warty noses. They have long, spindly fingers (the better to cast spells with). When they aren't off on midnight broom rides, black cats in tow, they are at home in their caves or cottages, hunched over boiling cauldrons of frog-knuckle broth, mumbling mumbo jumbo, preparing to hex some poor unsuspecting prince or princess. These are the pictures that come to mind when we think of witches. But where do these pictures come from? In order to understand this, it is necessary to understand where witches come from. For this, we must go back to the earliest time in human history, to the Old Stone Age, when people lived in caves, hunting animals and gathering food. The most important person in the Stone Age household (or cavehold) was the woman. She tended the all-important cave fire. She kept track of the seasons. She remembered which animals went to graze where at what time of year. She was in charge of gathering food, so she knew all about vegetables and herbs. She knew what herbs brought down swelling, what herbs eased pain, what herbs caused drowsiness. It is not surprising, then, that the Stone Age people worshipped a mother goddess. But the Stone Age came to a close. People learned to use tools. They left the caves and built towns and cities. They came to worship new religions, gods and goddesses of Olympus and, later, a single God and his son, Jesus Christ. By now, mothers had long since stopped passing on to daughters the knowledge of herbs. The people who had most of the knowledge about the natural world were scientists. Meanwhile, there remained a few isolated communities of people who were, so to speak, left over from the Old Stone Age. They continued to worship the Old Religion of the mother goddess, keeping their religion alive by meeting on nights of the full moon, to dance and to gather herbs. Because of their midnight meetings, their knowledge of herbs, their ability to disappear into the woods in the blink of an eye, the people in the city came to call these people fairies and goblins and little people and, most commonly, witches. Much as they scoffed at witches, city people went to witches for help, when they needed an herb to cure asthma, a love potion, an herb to cure the sickness of cattle. Sometimes, they went to witches for poisonous herbs which they might use to kill the cattle of a rival farmer, to do away with an enemy. It is the few witches who gave poison to their customers who earned all witches an ugly reputation. As soon as people learned that witches actually could hurt living things, they began to blame all sorts of mishaps on witches, from crop-killing frosts to the death of chickens.

So next Halloween, when you are carving your jack-o-lantern, or listening to a spooky story, set aside a moment in memory of good witches.

November has 30 days

November has come, and with it the first frost. The trees are bare. It is a good time to collect dried things: dried seed pods, dried flowers, dried grains. It is a good month for homebodies, for lovers of the hearth and home and family. It is a good time to sit by a fire and talk with cousins and uncles and aunts and brothers and sisters, to sit at long tables and feast, to watch the sky and wait for that first, very special snow.

Elections

One of the most precious rights of humans is the right to elect the leader of our choice. Equally important is the right to keep that vote a secret, if we choose to. Ancient Romans voted on matters of state: a black pebble meant "yes," a white one meant "no." Later, the French voted by writing their choice on paper, balling it up so that no one could read it, and casting it into a big pot. The paper was called *balla*, from which we get the words, "to cast your ballot." In 1851, Francis Dutton invented the first truly secret ballot. Nowadays, many countries have voting machines. The machine is in a booth. It will not record your vote unless you first draw the curtain so that no one but you and the machine will know how you voted.

Symbols

Chrysanthemum is November's flower. It grows in most colors except blue and purple.

The birthstone is **topaz,** standing for fidelity.

Sagittarius

the archer
Nov. 22 - Dec. 22 

People born under the sign of Sagittarius are sporting types. They are patient and loving with children and excellent at housekeeping. The world marvels at the generosity and honesty of the average Sagittarian.*

Famous people born in Sagittarius:
Walt Disney, founder of Disney studios, maker of Mickey Mouse, born 1901.
Mark Twain, writer, humorist, born 1835.
Ludwig Van Beethoven, German composer, born 1770.

Friends' birthdays:

* Remember to swallow with grain of salt, when necessary.

November Past

"Dr. Livingstone, I presume?"
When the Scottish missionary and explorer had been long missing, reporter Stanley journeyed into deepest Africa in search of him. He found Livingstone in November of 1871.

First on the Turf
Rutgers and Princeton played the first intercollegiate football game in America at New Brunswick, New Jersey in November of 1869.

"Four score and seven years ago. . . ."
Lincoln delivered the now famous Gettysburg address in November of 1863.

Holidays

Election Day—first Tuesday
Will Rogers' Day (in Oklahoma)—November 4
Veterans' Day—November 11
Elizabeth Cady Stanton Day—November 12
Thanksgiving Day—fourth Thursday

And

USE THIS SPACE TO WRITE IN YOUR FAVORITE NOVEMBER DAYS.

Not quite a year had passed since the Mayflower anchored off the rocky coast of New England. That first winter had been full of hardship. Sickness and starvation had wiped out over half the settlers. Yet, when spring came, the survivors refused to give up and return to England. They had come to the New World to stay. The Indians were there to help them put in the first crop. They showed the Pilgrims how to till the rocky soil, how to fertilize the crops

with fish, and when to harvest. The first crop was 20 acres of corn, six acres of barley and six acres of peas. The first summer was wet and sunny, ideal growing conditions. After the autumn harvest, the settlers were able to store away enough food to see them through the winter. In December, Governor Bradford called for a holiday celebration. The Pilgrims were not much for celebrations, but this was a special occasion. They had fasted together and starved together and survived together. Now was the time to feast together and give thanks to the Lord, and to the Indians for their generous assistance. A runner was sent to Mount Hope, inviting Chief Massasoit and his braves to come share in the feast. Meanwhile, the settlers hunted partridge and wild turkey and wood pigeon. They baked golden pumpkin pies and loaves of barley and corn bread. There were nets of fresh fish from the bay and baskets of wild plums and apples. Over 90 braves showed up for the feast, more than were expected, but there was food enough for all. Together they sat outside at long wooden tables beneath the trees. Between courses, the settlers showed the Indians how they marched in formation. The Indians showed the settlers how they danced. The next day, the braves went out and shot many deer, that the feast might continue into a second and third day. Never before had the sober Pilgrims enjoyed such a merry time.

December has 31 days

December is here
and it is holiday time in homes everywhere. December is best when the world is snowy and white, except for the bright, cheery green of the evergreen tree, the red and green of the holly bush. December is a time of giving, of making things, of decorating, of getting together and singing to celebrate the Winter Solstice.

Season's Greetings

Symbols

Holly is the flower for December. It has spiny leaves and bright red berries. The birthstone is **turquoise,** symbol of success.

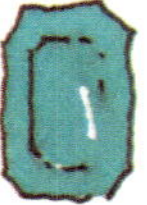

Capricorn

the goat
Dec. 22 - Jan. 20 ♑

People born under the sign of Capricorn are highly ambitious in business, and usually successful. Capricornians are secretive, economical, considerate, inventive and shy. They have a weakness for music.*

Famous people born in Capricorn:
Clara Barton, nurse and humanitarian, born 1821.
Joan of Arc, born 1412.
Benjamin Franklin, statesman, inventor, author of *Poor Richard's Almanack,* born 1706.

Friends' birthdays:

* Remember to swallow with grain of salt, when necessary.

Ken Marcus Daly

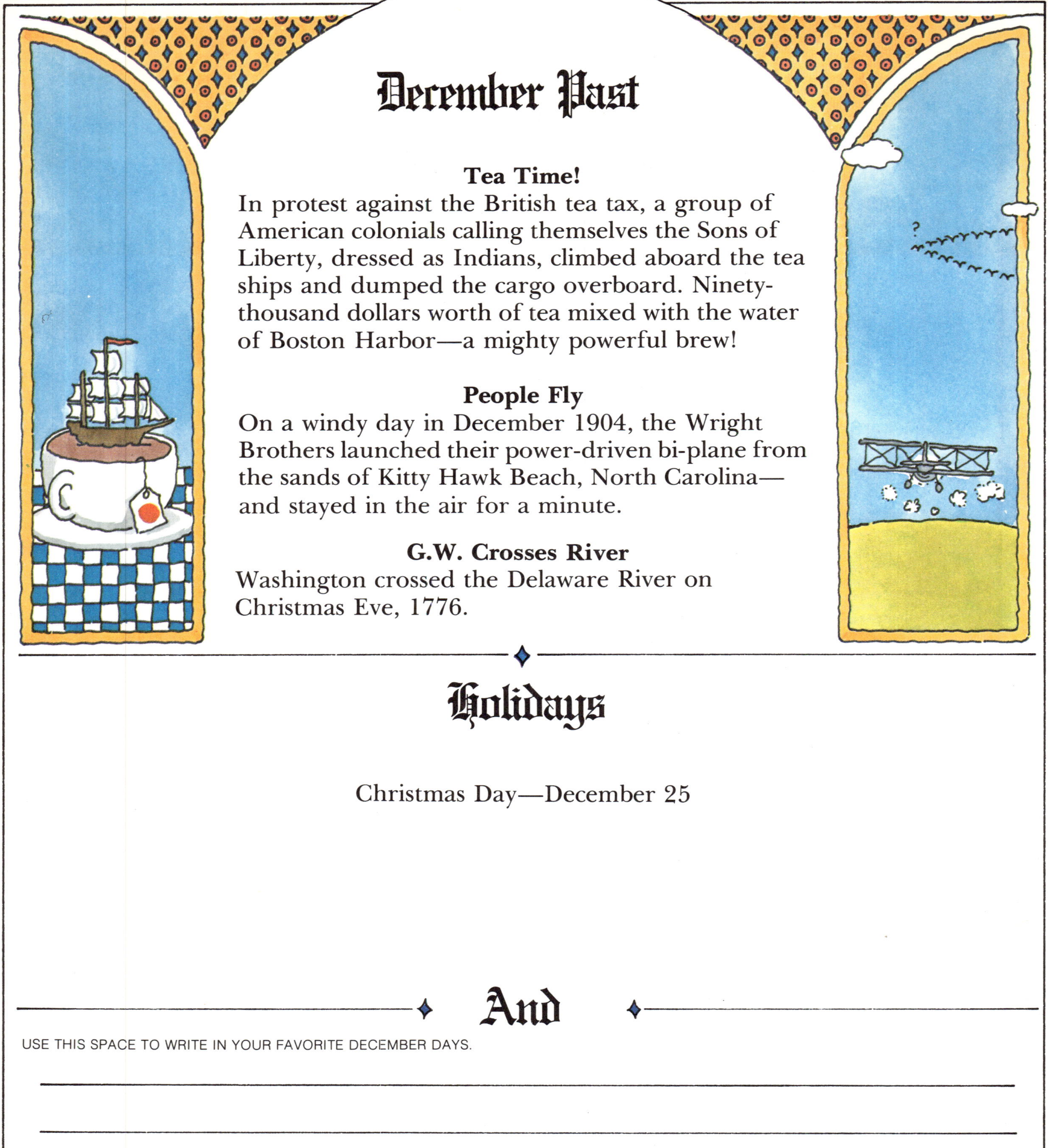

December Past

Tea Time!

In protest against the British tea tax, a group of American colonials calling themselves the Sons of Liberty, dressed as Indians, climbed aboard the tea ships and dumped the cargo overboard. Ninety-thousand dollars worth of tea mixed with the water of Boston Harbor—a mighty powerful brew!

People Fly

On a windy day in December 1904, the Wright Brothers launched their power-driven bi-plane from the sands of Kitty Hawk Beach, North Carolina—and stayed in the air for a minute.

G.W. Crosses River

Washington crossed the Delaware River on Christmas Eve, 1776.

Holidays

Christmas Day—December 25

And

USE THIS SPACE TO WRITE IN YOUR FAVORITE DECEMBER DAYS.

The Winter Solstice

In ancient Rome, every December 12, a priest stood before the temple of Saturn and called out, "Io, Saturnalia! Io Saturnalia!" So began the 12 days of the festival of Saturnalia. The Romans lit candles to Saturn, the god of the harvest. They decorated their houses with wreathes of laurel and evergreen. No one had to work. Everyone feasted and paraded and danced and exchanged gifts and made merry for 12 days.

The tribes of Germany, celebrated those same 12 days and nights in honor of the victory of the sun god and the south wind over winter and the storm god, destroyer of life. They gathered round roaring fires and toasted their good fortune with a spirited punch.

The Scandinavians, their ships icebound in the harbor for the winter, built a fire from an entire tree trunk. The fire warded off the dreaded Frost King. They drank a beverage called mead, and told ghost and werewolf stories.

The Druids, in what is now Great Britain, cut boughs of sacred mistletoe at the end of every December.

Comes a time every year, the time of the Winter Solstice, when people feel the urge to celebrate. This was as true in ancient times as it is today. Now, people may call the celebration by different names—Saturnalia or Christmas or Chanukah. They may attach different legends to it—the birth of Christ or the revolt of the Macabees or even Frost King. But the spirit of the celebration remains the same. And in the present day Christmas and Chanukah celebrations, can be seen traces of customs dating back to the dawn of civilization. So whether we light candles, or deck the halls with boughs of holly, the spirit we honor is the unconquerable spirit of life over death, of human kindness and love over cruelty and hatred, of light over darkness.

Celebrate!

Nowadays, more and more of us find ourselves spending the Winter Solstice going shopping and buying things. This holiday season, come away from the shopping centers and back to the home. Celebrate by making things and doing things. Who knows, maybe you will strike up your very own holiday traditions!

***Make bayberry candles.** Early American children made bayberry candles, and so can you. (Provided there are bayberry bushes in your vicinity.) Get some bayberries. Put them in a pot with water to cover and boil for an hour. Let cool; skim. The bayberry mixture is now ready. When you want to make candles, reheat the mixture. Cut wicks the height you want your candles, plus 8 inches. Tie the ends of the wicks to a pencil or long stick of wood. Pour the melted mixture into a tall, sturdy container at least as high as you want your candles to be. Then dip, dip, dip the wicks until your candles are the desired thickness.

***Bring in the Yule Log.** If you have a fireplace and an unusually large log of wood on the woodpile (a section of the trunk of a felled tree will do), attach ropes to it, put an old blanket beneath it, and drag it to the fireplace, singing as you come. "Bringing in the yule log" is a ceremony dating back to the ancient Celts.

***Trim the tree.** String cranberries and popcorn and dried fruits. Make cookies and hang them (eat them, too).

***Deck the Halls.** Make over-the-door decorations from evergreen boughs. Bring a little winter nature into the house with holly and mistletoe and other winter greens.

*Light a candle in the window.** Make candle arrangements in the windows, a sign of welcome to holiday visitors.

***Make "stained glass".** Make a mosaic design out of different colored pieces of crepe paper. Tape them to the window. Notice the effect when the light shines through!

***Make a centerpiece for the holiday table.**

***Make a wreath.** In ancient times, an evergreen wreath was a sign of triumph over biting winter cold. Bend a coathanger, or tie a soft willow branch into a circle. Tie onto the circular frame 6-inch sprays of different evergreens, all going in the same direction around the circle. Make a ribbon from fabric scraps. And remember, the ribbon doesn't always have to be red. Any bright color—even a pattern—is festive.

***Make a Wassail Bowl.** Mix up a combination of your favorite fruit juices. Pour it into a large punch bowl and put the bowl in a nest of evergreen and fruit. Invite the lords and ladies in to toast the holiday health and cheer, just as they did in Merry Old England.

***Sing carols** round the fire or simply sitting in a circle. The word "carol" comes from a word which means "to dance in a ring." Go to the music library and find some carols no one has heard before. Copy down the words of the new carols and put them in a decorative folder.

***Give gifts.** You can make gifts, or you can find gifts. A pinecone, a nicely-shaped rock, an interesting bit of driftwood—all natural "found" objects make splendid, special presents because you select them, and give them in a spirit of love.

SOUTH CIRCUMPOLAR CONSTELLATIONS
THE ALTAR
PAVO
TRIANGLE
OCTANS
TUCANA
CENTAURUS
COAL SACK
SOUTHERN CROSS
SOUTH POLE
HYDRUS
ACHERNAR
VOLANS
CARINA
DORADO